BOOK LEFT OPEN IN THE RAIN

BLACK SQUARE EDITIONS & THE BROOKLYN RAIL

book left open in the rain

BARRY SCHWABSKY

I can study rain.

ROBERT JOHNSON

CONTENTS

ACKNOWLEDGEMENTS

These poems were first published in the following magazines and online publications

Detroit: Telegraph — A Journal of Hence
How to Ring Bells With a Hammer
Again, Architecture

Dragonfire — Nude Beach Manifesto
Des Knaben Wunderhorn (Main Body)
Crickets, Inc.

Fieralingue — Diamond Replicas

GutCult — And One Will Be Sent to You As Well;
Sphere, Cone, Cylinder

Mirage #4/Period(ical) — "ways to make a man feel like an un-
employed hearse driver who had had a
little trouble with the higher powers"

Octopus — Immigrant, Little Orange Vendor, Bot

P.F.S. Post — Biblical Woman, Night of the Peacocks

Shampoo — Willing and Not Willing, Another Song

Sidereality Japanese Rug, Silent Plea (IX)

Tin Lustre Mobile Tephra

Titanic Operas Earthquake Weather, Other Music

Vanitas Transit, A Game of Return,
Inasmuch

West Wind Review After Dancing on the Bed,
From the Portuguese

"ways to make a man feel like an unemployed hearse driver who had had a little trouble with the higher powers" has been published with art by Hong Seung-Hye in the chapbook [ways] by Artsonje Center and Meritage Press, 2004

"Tephra" has been published as a chapbook by Black Square Editions, 2005

"Diary of a Poem" was first published in *History of a Painting/Storia di un quadro* with art by Maria Morganti, Edizioni Corraini, 2006

"Des Knaben Wunderhorn (Main Body)" has been published in *Rock and Shift* with art by Suzanne McClelland, Hard Press Editions with One Eye Pug, 2008

ANOTHER SONG

Suck the air from my mouth. Push it back
through my nostrils. Did I say
"Breathe?" You, my shrine ajar.
My cracked reliquary. Feeble heart. Even in

a poem beginning, "My heart aches,"
no one lets me down the way I want
or, in truth, knows how to press me
like the grass flattened beneath your sandal.

WILLING AND NOT WILLING

Viewed from God's balcony
the sky makes no sense
but evening air
gets pushy that way. Something's gone
and what remains? Open-air theater
of gorgeousness
and gloom. Occasion for painting's
rage and
death.
　　　Your saying
is what makes it so
(quoting "everybody will help you")
as thought keeps driving further toward its fires
but lightning's not meant to strike twice
in one face, I mean
the one remembered
as a favorite book with pages now brittle
for having once been left open
in the rain.

EARTHQUAKE WEATHER

No, but unseasonable air
touches you
outside. Hangs
fireworks in trees, then way past
to the treasury of the middle eye
forgotten – forgotten beauty
whose vergence
displays death
correctly. Eye muscles:
superior, lateral, inferior, oblique.
Somewhere a tremor
sets off. Then
flick. Already in the face
you were born with, a powerful
surface, someone's usual
invitation to try spotting the moon
in clear, rippling water.

CRICKETS, INC.

A gradual mood writes itself
and no idea where it's going
beyond thank-your-stars
and one lonely voice all lost to you
even all the shadows on your hands.

Trespass, pilgrim,
toward and away from me
the one who broke ranks
with the dead, sprawling classes
out of use. Making
free with syntax they say
they want to get me high
and they do; I definitely
heard the ghosts singing and this
was the sound they made.

She stood back from her life
to admire it: diaphanous
among ancientries,

palpable
smoke. Slipped off,
he noticed, it shows
less naked. Twilight smiles

the god we worship reciprocally
as your eyes exhale
twilight. I hear it, your
face music. How open the eyes

become. Only let your mouth
collect its
carnal fee, oh Juno.

Our posthumous life
– cancelled. Yet
still we shared

our plague
of frogs. Delicious. But now
sky thickens, its shine

soft, softest. Sounds
divest. Even rain
spies that garden, the red there

under wind
all gray with remembered
words, cushioned tread.

JAPANESE RUG

Because I am unshaken in my belief that the dead are dead.

ANTAL SZERB

She wants me to read her brown, then her green, then her cream.
    To read
her preferred order. Read her lips. Her crescent moon, newest
    whip. She wants me
to read her riot act, her lopped promises, preferred disorder.
    Thank you: for un-
undoing recognition (your word) as metaphor (technically clear).
    You can't cross out
a full stop or capitalize the desired reader, your cross-country
divinity. Nationwide! And absolutely
prose. Color: Black on sky. But only when I read her swarms, her
    tricky honey-
gathering procedures, her pursed signifiers, her cream.

LITTLE ORANGE VENDOR

Does a star? I mean for
the minimum scene, the one

she puts in her sketches, this artist
who is from the interior

of never give the words
a second chance. Wide awake

main sleep, totemic
in underbrush, the color

that lost capacity to call
a world from certain traces

more substantially than spiderwebs.

SILENT PLEA (IX)

Notice the way I notice
you. The way my mouth would notice
the nape of your neck, unseen.
Sit down with me before
disappearing,
please. While red light
darkens, draw me to
your broken surface. Have you ever held
the wrong breath? The moon
tilts against
our not yet under-
standing.
          Turn that star down
a notch. Now work your way toward
what difference what
you want to feel. Toward your beds
of wildflowers again. Toward your
breath of grass
ago. But watch
what you wish for. Is it all over
my face? Then keep shining
my moon.

BIBLICAL WOMAN

One eye milk, the other eye honey.

OTHER MUSIC

She liked him now, as she liked a memory.

D.H. LAWRENCE

We joined the army
of never, met death
by extracts. But in

the leafy shade of what
hesitated eye
or pitched to whose

crucified lips? Dear
sunlit junk: I hunt
your traces even

in perfume
of rose petals – the red ones
of the variety "Deep

Secret," to be precise.
Their soundless waves
of live or die. Please,

deep breather, don't
melt. Love knows
fuck-all about love.

So we tortured
a couple of shadows.
Go get anger and dig me

a love six feet deep.

A GAME OF RETURN

Thanks to one of her some our garments
of self-portrayal kept falling past
a surface of water. Worlds hidden
outside myself without description – whole streets
of once-beautiful buildings overwhelmed by heavenly
theater or antagonistic nature. "Which part of beauty do you
like best?" she asked. Memory of intimate
fractions: a folded wall. She explained, "This fish
is the metaphor of a woman without gravity, likewise its wetness
signifies the marriage bed." What once touched her skin
is now engraved shadow. Her grassy
feet are not for these surroundings. Let the shadow
of this woman be cast in paper only
to come alive in present light.

IMMIGRANT

Certain days
I used to think of leaving
the East Country, now not even
a darting memory – just a hole in
the sky before which
grain elevators hang
nailed. I drank wine
of immoral bouquet: sea foam,
midday drizzle, ash of poppies, copperas,
mustard. Then I stopped arriving
and the eye-burn
stopped happening. Still the blind
sky stands out
anonymous
with birds
of raw meat. Breath
changes color. I call the window closer
but it won't come. The eye yaws, flooded
with dreams of targets
and insomniac
sheets. A funeral
with interruptions:

"Organ, shut up!" sing the birds
before the stony minute turns its face
the other way round.

ii

"ways to make a man look like an unemployed hearse driver who had had a little trouble with the higher powers"

MARGUERITE YOUNG

I

In a poem of all mistaken beginnings
or the hair music of your recurrent brushing

an endless pleasure seeps through
cupped hands. Slightly unsightly, some feet

might drip with bare song
the tuning of an unseen instrument

and then I brushed you
with one person's misdirected kisses.

But avant-couriers in tatters
slack with sun and air, sorry

yet enduring silent, and with closed eyes?
An endless middle of muddled colors,

it was whispered, ripples slanted tree shadows
on this page, left intentionally blank.

II

One man, one vote, and both possibly spoiled
or wasted on streaming eye contact. Alright, but

broken in so many places,
the misdirected kisses I mean, the money shot

could only have blanched in their glare.
Push. It's a hard lever to push

once everything new flashes
old once more: second loves

love best. Semistarved
but otherwise ordinary though painfully far

from post-ironic, I'm happy
you can read it too—I mean,

this page left intentionally blank
beneath the reluctant seepage of my eye.

III

Where are you? Outside the burnt library
of all-purpose similes such as

fog latched hard to a mountainside
the way you talked it up before lapping snowfall

or (perfect circumvention) autumns
of fruit bruised perfectly as you still dream

to taste it, dripping. Where are you?
Far outside where blush-colored stars

weigh in torn like we used to be
your battery run low or voice growing

sweetly lazy, please. Soon.
This page left intentionally blank

and promoted to some ropey transcendence
would also be worth burning, sure.

IV

Sonata for sewing machine. The signal processing
makes it, obviously. Like telling

secrets all night as a way of making love
tacitly. Or rather, tacit. Haven't you ever

pressed the right key into the wrong
door in the right hotel the wrong night?

Sorry, that was someone else's holiday.
But something else you might want to know:

how words trail off to the point
where you write them idly

on a page left intentionally blank
and even get them spelled right sometimes

as if the lyrics to a naked song ever seep down
that same casual storage to where you levitate.

V

Yes, we shared a lot of reminiscences.
Like hands rubbing two sides of a pear,

ripe and bruised. Then aired grievances
we never knew we had. Open-mouthed

too, as if you'd never hushed the school
of hidden kisses. In precious time

withheld such sweet slovenly days as make
burnt ends meet before an ugly cloud

disperses peacefully, soaks deep
into a page left intentionally blank.

Yes, it was the wrong hotel. But it was
the right key. Oh thank you, Jesus.

Let me hear an "Amen." It's on a timer,
the kind of light you can only switch on.

VI

Was it just preaching to the choir when she
kept breathing in, out, in, out, in, out, in....

or as a child's tooth may dangle by a thread
will your idea of pleasure hang poignant

before falling with the tiniest breath from
your mouth? We've seen those French farces before,

his lover hidden under the bed, hers
waiting patiently inside the wardrobe.

But that page left intentionally blank
within the luminous wreckage of our

blasted contract is what protects us from meaning
that another shot of good

memory can pack it up smartly
and keep washing in, out, in, out, in, out, in...

VII

A second honeymoon's the name
our twin sirens Necessity and Danger

give the love they also called
their dreamwork, their lovely toy.

Like daylight their kisses wax and wane
but seasonally. And masturbating they express

their desire that you never stop reading
this page left intentionally blank

in the intentionally open folder
of a black and troubled memory.

The tremulous flanks of a small
envious beast keep heaving

and we'd best start thinking burnt
offerings in the past or pluperfect tense.

VIII

Shake my ribs a little please
but from the inside. You like questions

with no right answers? Try playing
that song recalling what you thought

when you heard it first but you won't. Ever.
Spacious light cuts across the surface

of a page left intentionally blank
where someone's life ends beautifully

or not at all. A conspiracy of good feelings
might appease the prettiest pain

ever seen. I closed
the big brown eyes of shame

that read the story of snow but you know
what? It was very, very something.

IX

Fertility and other stories told
in once-contracted eyes now dilate

in the shadows of a shadow
where closer music listens in

to strangely muddled colors
wet a page left intentionally blank

with something half past endless.
Pleasure? To be continued:

Cut. The trouble with being
is not wanting to until

we hear the children listen hard
to stuttered music. A face breaks

into private laughter. Ask my
bones if they can please you.

X

Behind brushed hair catch a whiff
of possible futures. Belly yours.

Again. Mouth open sky.
Again. Wet fingers wet corners

of a page left intentionally blank.
Is this your body? Membrane

soaked with almosts. Delicious
blood or an eye unstuck. Begin

generic shadow weather,
Mrs. Blue Skies — translationese

for music pushed through blown
speakers. Slow-burning when I do you

this ode to distraction, invisible
and certified real as the day.

XI

We haven't been here since the last time
we were here. Wasted and a bit

out of breath we know what's coming
a page left intentionally blank.

Didn't I know you once before
this language broke

inside me? Mouth stuffed
with lies I never got to tell? You turn

a face daylight lined with sleep
growling. Morning falls behind

my eyes. Door to the sky,
open, leaving something bright inside,

a face that stripped the soul off me
and loved what's left.

XII

These morning worlds take longer to read
than write. Study for skin:

this page left intentionally blank
or caught in an echo where rain heard

loveless lullabies puddle under eaves
where random noises nest. You want

to replace existing
ways? You're the one I.... Well,

you'll find out. A weather obsessive
iced up in dormant analogies,

I want my animal rights
but now: bend down

to see those stars go quietly idle
in light I'm dripping all over you.

XIII

I own just so many words, mostly written
on this page left intentionally blank —

all God's faults on display. Red wine
would be your weapon of choice

when poetry is no longer legible
in the mild light of disinclined eyes

like the painting bitten by a man
of which (of whom?) we once read

in tears. My corrupted eyes read off
the timestamps inflicted on them

as responsibilities
become less. Lovely word,

disinclined. One word saves space
in the slow strength of another.

XIV

A page left intentionally blank
like sky remanded thoughtfully

clouded behind its peering
starlessness contracts

however spacious and not in envy
of the branching loves and flowering

sadness below
whose time attenuates

like lines of a poem that's forgotten
half its lines or desires them

to be written incessantly
over not to forget

itself reminds you
of a song's mistaken beginnings.

XV

A severe colorist makes her presence known
wanting a sequestered blue

to trap facts
of dark honeyed vagueness,

image that now belongs
to another eye

unmoved
from its secret notebook

whose place is immaterial:
speechless words, afflicted

pleasures, if not without
strength though having repaired

to where you, Carol, keep opening
to deep sound after all.

iii

TEPHRA

I

Signal: Went kneeling under
                            (banners
of silken laundry)
                colors decocted

from piles dealt
                    me
like cards (royal flush

if I'm right in seeing the light
falling moist)

from the eyes
                    (of darkened distance:
light falling out of itself)

the color of laughter, memory at the crux
of a shared

                    misunderstanding. Since then
we share   51
        the name: Solitude.

11

As I keep hearing so clearly
(what unfolded eyes would sing)

I swear your eyes will never once lack
(nocturnal song to swell a dark throat)

(even) my accented translation
                              (or false transcription
(mute hunger to hear it))

stirs with (leafing) joy
you read folded
                    among lost pleasures and

rediscovered distances
            (safer)

in the secret face
I'll (never not) turn
                    (to yours).

III

But it would be your breath
(braking tender into my skull)

and there lodge
in the lost of it, a dream
                    (of time)

upheld
by supporting hands at the nape

of my logic, otherwise weak
— would be your breath

furred like peaches in
                    (the poem
of)
          my mouth: taste...

IV

More than just correctly language
(with) the also-conventional body of love in mind

and the pollution of night
                            (swimmy) in my ear
still-untouched misunderstanding

written on pages and pages
                                (of silence)
that find themselves forward

into sadness: let go of your breath, let spread
the finger-trees of your greeting.

V

Face that unfolded my face
(to the sun's plain nourishment)

in place of the thought
that laughter falls falls falls falls falls falls falls

without touch bottom
(in the absolute right to hunger and cold).
                                        Did I

mention thighs? Whose constant appearance
advances
            (in all directions)

toward lost matter or the undersigned
(shed carapace

or carnal blossom)
                    fallen
in the spirit-hole? – Hey Apollo!

VI

Seeing that words are (poetry)
when you recognize them

(at least as figures to a text unfolding nightly)
out of earshot. Seeing space
                              (wadding up)

behind our backs. How is painting
thought? Cruising the galleries in
                              (the intimate embarrassment, I say,

of)
        an eye turned inside out
                              (like the glove
my hand could be)
                    in yours.

VII

Impatience faster than music
we planted small animals on the kissed-up face of earth

— and daughters (of parenthesis)
                                    to later
milk them, express dew

of their bodies. We call that love,
the virginal. It would be
                                    (enough if only

weather took our place)
                                    before
bright coinage we'll start to exchange

— no: if only weather took place behind you
                                                        (in the keep of
(in the color of) waiting space)

(one we'll always fill)
past wording.

VIII

Action immobilizes. It loses you
your skin. To serve: to be the will

of another.
                        (You don't
believe me? Undress).

DES KNABEN WUNDERHORN (MAIN BODY)

This living number before me
the pressure of their fingers
leans deeply to ground connection
and gloss brightens
arterial
her dress seam.

☾

"In air I'd probably listen to birds!"
awake from sin's sleep
she coops up like a dream.

☾

No blood, no hair
and that's still another step.

☾

I want to touch down by you soon
bright day bent only to itself
lures a beautiful ghost to the window
I threw it to the grass.

⸲

Abridged messages
written in the sheets there
a bed with no springs
main headers

probably to a new song
as chamfered out at Easter.

⸲

Winter desires
a future with fur lining;
how long does it learn seams?

❧

A skirt imprinted
with words and pictures remains
the blue sky tent
a little fear mistook
how bright the moon would seem to us
carved canaries.

❧

The canal floats erring lights
and there it was around midnight
eyes powered out, made us a deep grave
directly we tuned the sound

you tender fiddle
fedback, my wicked skin
for all that we wait.

DIAMOND REPLICAS

Words for women and other writers

the eye unsilenced

an elaborate (but unscratchy) necklace

dawn stirs in one nostril

birds imprisoned in an eye

her tears go flying home

unspangled

this sprig of loss

known forward into

iris recognition

conversation of sweat

the door shuts the house

with pointless conviction

your whispering campaign against my eyes

songlessness, or rather sunglasses

and in for it:

– a map of how to lose your way
– the door of departure
– not two breaths to my name
– it makes me its own
– colors your eye

He found a poem trapped
in its own light
the ghost at its back
just dusk, a plunging silhouette
launched toward

the hang of your phonetic eye

a divine disproportion

shove another hour up the clock

pluck late music from a single string

what unholy racket

the sky makes even less sense now

grass bends before each wind

all the air in my nostrils

how open your mouth could be

she offered a whisper

setting words to a face

remember stone heat

we speak in overlap

tasting brightly

the surprise of the ever-later

a voice asleep

in the middle of early.

v

DIARY OF A POEM

Prose refuted:

struck, the blank hour stays
struck – an indoor resolution
and most merciless of all
the colors we tweaked together

prose refuted:

rumor slides across rumor
each remembers to search my morning suspect

she loves the sound of breaking chains.

℃

Prose refuted:

struck, the hour stays
struck – an indoor resolution
and most merciless of all
your face made me noisy

the essay melted
in the blood mine
as if we had any choice

prose refuted:

that rumor enjambed on
a plaque in the red-brick museum of loneliness
you need so much research to make it beautiful
but please don't make me say it.

ℭ

Prose refuted:

next best thing to wordless
the violet day hammers along
and most merciless of all
impossible to have been present without

taking part
in those colors

prose refuted:

God sleeps in his Word
get flung out of pretty
you need so much research to make it beautiful
but please don't make me say it.

℃

Prose refuted:

struck, the next best thing to wordless
the essay melted
and makes you want to crash
what sky-blue distance wrote

prose refuted:

so if I had a diary
even critics pass away
they want to search my morning suspect

she loves the sound of breaking chains.

℃

Prose refuted:

the essay melted
a space to peer into and lean
out of

thrones, dominions
in the casual sense

prose refuted:

God sleeps in his grassy Word
whose angel folds me carefully

the colors we tweaked together
his outtakes and bloopers.

¢

Prose refuted:

rumor slides across rumor
I sank into it but forgot to drown

this canary borne repeating
on fast clouds

toward prose refuted:

go forth little saffron bird
toward inquorate nights of poetry
your rumor
more than gone.

¢

Prose refuted:

in this bronze museum
Rembrandt, lift me up to golden failure
let grief pacification false memory
drift outside the book

prose refuted:

don't kiss
all she wants is
your every forgiveness

let's get our pretty rumors
in the sunlight
more than gone

lipidic colors
prose refuted.

vi

Nocturnal parallels
with evasive shadows
to which expectations may be buttoned

the object of any and every couple
become mere music
you're the singer to a corpse.

BOT

You can cry until your eyeballs rust but
never break a sky
trussed in violet conversation
(your lucky couch professor)

pale conversation
where telephones keep ringing
to get me some.

NUDE BEACH MANIFESTO

Set personal files
beside the tribute pit
summertime being automatic
you mainly drive the body clean

my burnt honey thesis voided
or brained back into itself with excuses
a double sense of berries
enters the soap opera world of dry cleaners at night
(part illegible) along Lee Miller's neck.

SPHERE, CONE, CYLINDER

In obvious depiction
lie swimming landscapes
wilted colors
and embassies of the change of state

our Persephone
to the dented loss of sleep
in a cute way
that painting is a too-clumsy object

that can only cure time
as it will never change
though maybe elements of what we would recognize as star glass

again curses cast into gloom
as a fresh summer warning
and our fingers have no fuses.

HOW TO RING BELLS WITH A HAMMER

for Pipilotti Rist and Tom Texas Holmes

Distracted in a rain of minnows
dropping in from clouds that have already disappeared
you lit toward unexpired aesthetic finality
sorry, stormed by swelling gods, thundering

betimed in harsh trees "stay metal" sensing
optical anarchy in these peopled shadows
later call you God's own darling
and wait to hear the bronze to go crack.

TRANSIT

Disassembled flame
"moving at summer's pace"
how we kiss tunes straight
until they sound like practice
float a rhythm over pennywise drones
the ionized outer cone conducts

Venus crosses sun – amazing pictures
that clock was exactly right
a poem whose subject so transcendently nondescript
was always just somewhere
however wronged

decriminalized, let's keep it cruel
the poor can only smoke
we'll make like trustafarians in the tropic of ease.

FROM THE PORTUGUESE

The extreme reach of alphabet
whose river repeats itself
holding in warm mouthfuls of simplicity
the tabloid brightness of that hand

museum passersby
stopped to make a poem out of saying something
torched
to rest alive in its glow.

AGAIN, ARCHITECTURE

Your churches, immensely vain
some music exhaled in a flash of bird's-wing
only to be heard after the fact
as abandoned silence

Hello, she lamented
and the sun went raw
into eyes of absent color
sweetcore smudged
without Vaseline

flatten this more-than-first of days
a word expunged in the flesh.

NIGHT OF THE PEACOCKS

Just in from the stars
and already my soul birds
taking black literally
shriek past sudden cinders of attention

break the seal of breathing light
she paints by flicking her eyelashes

escaped peacocks
watching our free movies in the street.

INASMUCH

Withdrawn like a god fed on lilies
crossing over into myself
in breath stained with images
I'll take time to tell the truth

that day scatters, night collects
crickets creak like used-up thoughts
between facing
mirrors light spreads wings

and all I need is air
but in homemade thunder another joy fades away.

Barry Schwabsky was born in Paterson, New Jersey, and presently lives in London. His previous collection is *Opera: Poems 1981-2002* (Meritage Press).

Book Left Open in The Rain is printed in an edition of seven hundred fifty copies by Thomson-Shore of Dexter, Michigan. The text is set in Rialto, a typeface designed by df Type of Austria. Duc de Berry appears throughout.